HANDSHAKE

STUDY GUIDE

Published by Arrows & Stones

Cover design: Sara Young
Cover photo: Brenton Stanley

ISBN: 978-1-960678-47-8   1 2 3 4 5 6 7 8 9 10

Printed in the United States of America

HANDSHAKE

WHAT THE GREAT DO THAT OTHERS DON'T

STUDY GUIDE

CHRIS SONKSEN

STUDY GUIDE

ARROWS &
STONES

CONTENTS

THE CHOICE OF CONFIDENCE

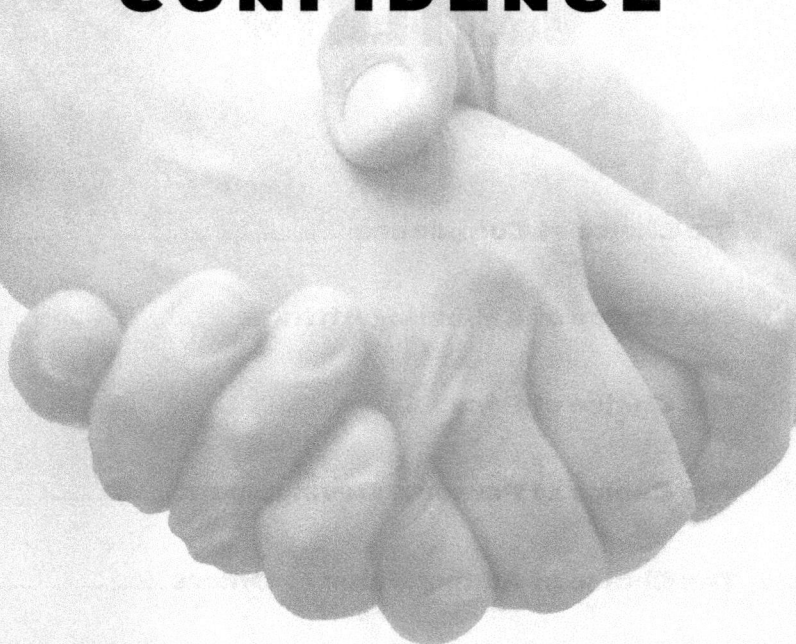

Greatness is not an inheritance.

As you read Chapter I: "The Choice of Confidence" in **HANDSHAKE**, reflect on the questions and scriptures.

REFLECT AND TAKE ACTION:

In your own words, how would you define confidence?

_____

_____

_____

_____

_____

_____

_____

_____

_____

_____

Who has exemplified confidence to you through their life and leadership? How did this influence you?

_____

_____

_____

_____

_____

_____

_____

_____

_____

_____

_____

_____

Are you confident? What area(s) of your life do you lack confidence in?

_____

_____

_____

_____

_____

_____

_____

_____

_____

Do you feel others see you as a confident individual? Why or why not?

_____

_____

_____

_____

_____

_____

_____

_____

_____

What areas of your life do you need to work on to achieve greatness?

_____

_____

_____

_____

_____

_____

_____

_____

_____

_____

Is it possible to be confident all the time, or does it depend on your situation? Explain your answer.

_____

_____

_____

_____

_____

_____

_____

_____

_____

How do you think confidence affects your output?

_____

_____

_____

_____

_____

_____

_____

_____

THE CHOICE OF A WINNING ATTITUDE

Decide what you want out of life;
look on the positive side; and never
give up until you achieve it.

READING TIME

As you read
Chapter 2:
"The Choice
of a Winning
Attitude" in

HANDSHAKE,

reflect on the
questions and
scriptures.

REFLECT AND TAKE ACTION:

How would you define an attitude? What are
the differences between a losing attitude
and a winning one?

_____
_____
_____
_____
_____
_____
_____
_____
_____
_____
_____

In what ways is your attitude a choice?

_____
_____
_____
_____
_____
_____
_____
_____
_____
_____

How is our attitude directly correlated to our success?

_____

_____

_____

_____

_____

_____

_____

_____

Are attitudes contagious? In what way? Is your attitude one that others would like to "catch"?

_____

_____

_____

_____

_____

_____

_____

_____

Who in your life always seems to have a good attitude? Do you recognize this rubbing off on you? Is the same true for anyone with a negative attitude?

_____

_____

_____

_____

_____

_____

_____

_____

_____

When you are presented with an obstacle or a less-than-ideal situation, how do you look at the problem? In a positive light or a negative one?

_____

_____

_____

_____

_____

_____

_____

_____

_____

_____

TAKE TIME TO GO THROUGH AND COMPLETE THE EXERCISES PROVIDED THROUGHOUT THIS CHAPTER.

CHAPTER 3

THE CHOICE
OF FOCUS

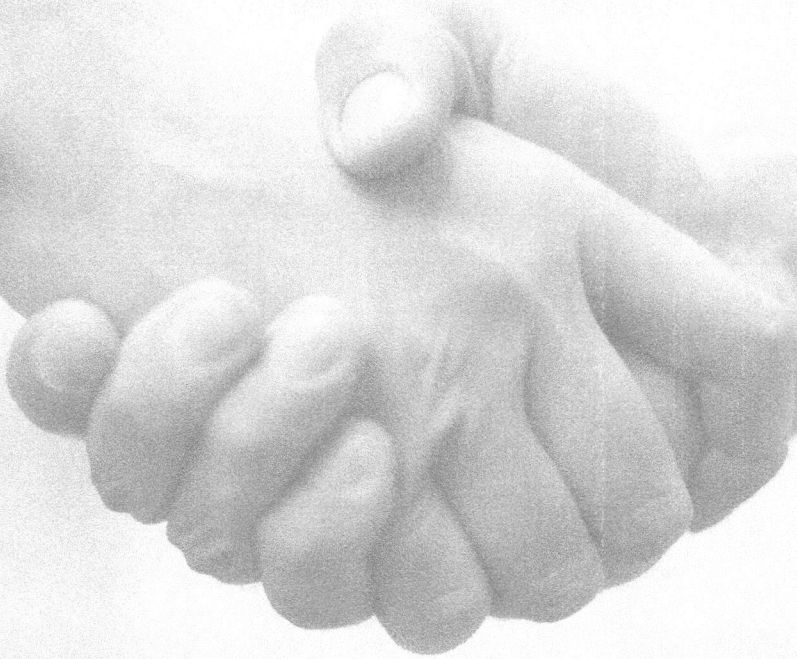

People cannot become great in
the future if they are not willing to
practice focus in the present.

READING TIME

As you read
Chapter 3:
"The Choice
of Focus" in

HANDSHAKE,

reflect on the
questions and
scriptures.

REFLECT AND TAKE ACTION:

What do you do to remain focused on your
goals and vision? When do you feel it's
difficult to focus?

_____

_____

_____

_____

_____

_____

_____

_____

_____

What distracts you from your main goals
in life? What excuses have you made or
currently are making to not pursue your
dreams and goals?

_____

_____

_____

_____

_____

_____

_____

_____

_____

What stands out to you from Jesse Owens's story in this chapter? How can you apply this to your own journey?

_____

_____

_____

_____

_____

_____

_____

_____

_____

What is focus? How will it help us in the pursuit of our goals?

_____

_____

_____

_____

_____

_____

_____

What happens when you are not focused on your goals?

_____

_____

_____

_____

_____

_____

_____

_____

_____

_____

In which of the four focus categories (no focus, unfinished, seasonal, and clear) would you place yourself, and why?

_____

_____

_____

_____

_____

_____

_____

_____

_____

Whom do you have in your life that can be your focus coach? Why did you choose them?

_____

_____

_____

_____

_____

_____

_____

_____

_____

THE CHOICE OF PERSONAL DEVELOPMENT

When personal growth becomes
part of your daily life, other avenues
of success are sure to follow.

READING TIME

As you read Chapter 4: "The Choice of Personal Development" in **HANDSHAKE**, reflect on the questions and scriptures.

REFLECT AND TAKE ACTION:

What do you do currently to invest in your personal development?

_____

_____

_____

_____

_____

_____

_____

_____

_____

_____

How would you define personal development? Why is this process important?

_____

_____

_____

_____

_____

_____

_____

_____

_____

Have you ever been unprepared to seize an opportunity that presented itself due to your neglecting personal development? Has this ever happened to someone you know? Describe the situation.

_____

_____

_____

_____

_____

_____

Have you ever created a growth plan? Take time to create or update a past growth plan using the guidelines provided in this chapter.

_____

_____

_____

_____

_____

_____

How can you set aside more time for personal growth in your daily life? What are some distractions you can get rid of?

_____

_____

_____

_____

_____

_____

Do you consider yourself to be teachable? Why or why not? Do you feel others would say the same?

_____

_____

_____

_____

_____

_____

_____

_____

From whom in your life can you learn? What can they teach you?

_____

_____

_____

_____

_____

_____

_____

_____

What areas of your life do you feel you need to grow the most in?

_____

_____

_____

_____

_____

_____

_____

_____

CHAPTER 5

THE CHOICE OF ADDING VALUE TO OTHERS

When you determine to be "others"
minded, you have made a decision
that will alter your life.

READING TIME

As you read Chapter 5: "The Choice of Adding Value to Others" in HANDSHAKE, reflect on the questions and scriptures.

REFLECT AND TAKE ACTION:

In what ways can you add value to those around you? Your spouse? Your children? Employees and coworkers? Friends?

_____
_____
_____
_____
_____
_____
_____
_____
_____
_____
_____

How often do you make an effort to add value to others?

_____
_____
_____
_____
_____
_____
_____
_____
_____
_____

What are the different ways you benefit from adding value to others? Explain each answer.

_____

_____

_____

_____

_____

_____

_____

_____

Which of the lessons learned from Howard Schultz stands out to you? How can you apply this to your daily life?

_____

_____

_____

_____

_____

_____

_____

_____

_____

When has someone added value to you? How did this make you feel?

_____

_____

_____

_____

_____

_____

_____

_____

_____

Who is the first person you'll add value to? When and how will you do it?

_____

_____

_____

_____

_____

_____

_____

_____

Have you ever felt like you needed to wait before you poured into others? Explain your answer.

_____

_____

_____

_____

_____

_____

_____

_____

_____

THE CHOICE OF CHARACTER

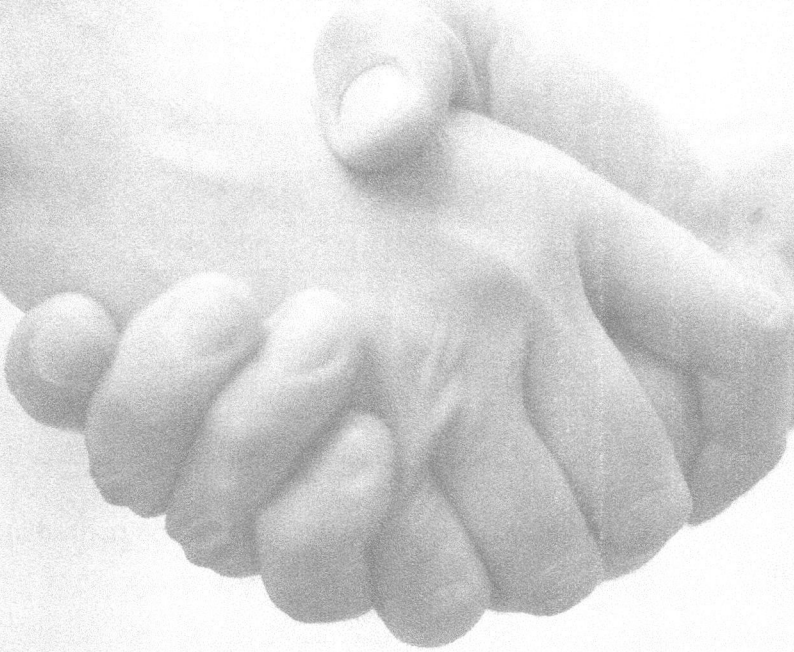

Character is what is inside of you; it's
who you are when no one is looking.

READING TIME

As you read Chapter 6: "The Choice of Character" in HANDSHAKE, reflect on the questions and scriptures.

REFLECT AND TAKE ACTION:

In your own words, what is the difference between character and reputation?

_____

_____

_____

_____

_____

_____

_____

_____

_____

_____

_____

How would you describe your character? Would those in your life say the same?

_____

_____

_____

_____

_____

_____

_____

_____

_____

_____

Are you the same person no matter the people you are (or are not) with?

_____

_____

_____

_____

_____

_____

_____

What are the four benefits that follow making character a foundation of your life?

_____

_____

_____

_____

_____

_____

_____

Of the lessons listed about Coach John Wooden, which do you need to work on most? Explain your answer.

_____

_____

_____

_____

_____

_____

_____

_____

Is your conscious clear, or do you need to confess something to someone?

_____

_____

_____

_____

_____

_____

_____

Are there any areas of your life that people may not trust you in? What are they? How can you work on your character in these areas?

_____

_____

_____

_____

_____

_____

_____

COMMIT TO BEING A PERSON OF INTEGRITY AND REACH OUT TO MAKE AMENDS WITH ANYONE YOU MAY HAVE HURT IN THE PAST.

THE CHOICE OF THINKING BIG

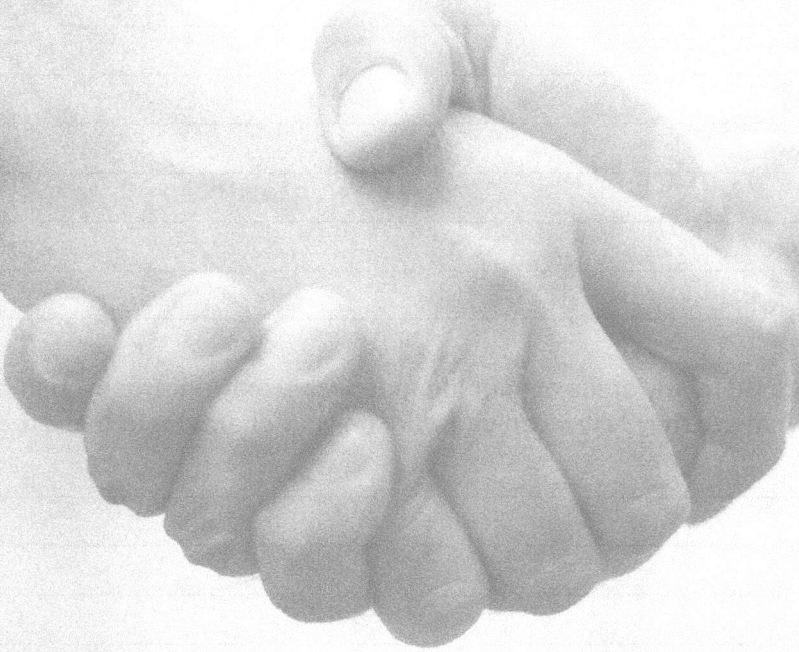

That's what thinking big will do
for you; it will shape your future
into an image of success.

READING TIME

As you read Chapter 7: "The Choice of Thinking Big" in **HANDSHAKE**, reflect on the questions and scriptures.

REFLECT AND TAKE ACTION:

Do you think big? Have you always thought this way, or did it take work and intentionality?

_____

_____

_____

_____

_____

_____

_____

_____

_____

_____

What are some of your biggest dreams? Why these?

_____

_____

_____

_____

_____

_____

_____

_____

_____

_____

Whom do you have on your team that can help you in your pursuit of this dream?

_____

_____

_____

_____

_____

If no one is on your team currently, whom in your life can you recruit to help?

_____

_____

_____

_____

_____

When have you thought small? Did you think you were thinking small in the moment or only retrospectively?

_____

_____

_____

_____

_____

How can you think even bigger in your current situation? What can you believe, pursue, and attain with God's assistance?

_____

_____

_____

_____

_____

_____

What rewards follow big thinking? When have you seen any of
these in your life?

_____

_____

_____

_____

_____

How does thinking big force teamwork and give you influence?

_____

_____

_____

_____

_____

What are some obstacles in life that are blocking you from
dreaming big? List all that apply.

_____

_____

_____

_____

_____

CHAPTER 8

THE CHOICE
OF COURAGE

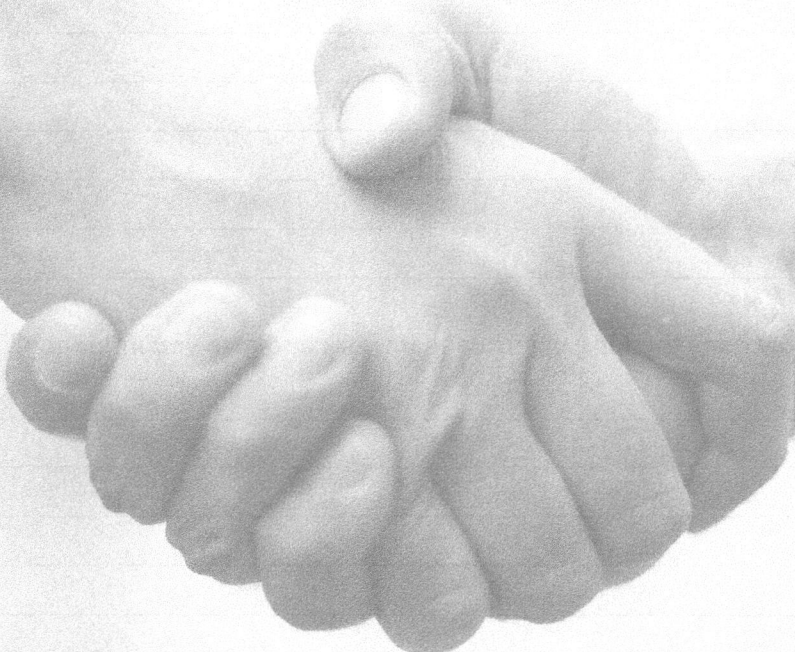

Courage is easier when you decide
your belief and principles upfront
and then stick with them.

READING TIME

As you read
Chapter 8:
"The Choice
of Courage" in

HANDSHAKE,

reflect on the
questions and
scriptures.

REFLECT AND TAKE ACTION:

In your own words, define courage and its significance.

_____

_____

_____

_____

_____

_____

_____

_____

_____

_____

What area of your life is holding you back? How might courage help you in this area?

_____

_____

_____

_____

_____

_____

_____

_____

_____

_____

_____

Can fear and courage be present at the same time? Explain your answer.

_____

_____

_____

_____

_____

_____

_____

When have you shown courage in the face of fear or uncertainty? How did this affect the situation?

_____

_____

_____

_____

_____

_____

_____

What is courage based upon? Where does it originate?

_____

_____

_____

_____

_____

_____

In what areas of your life is courage needed? Have you demonstrated courage in each of these areas?

_____

_____

_____

_____

_____

_____

_____

Have you ever had to stand alone in order to stand up for what is right? How did this make you feel? What did you learn?

_____

_____

_____

_____

_____

_____

_____

What do you feel a lack of courage could be holding you back from?

_____

_____

_____

_____

_____

_____

THE CHOICE OF VISION

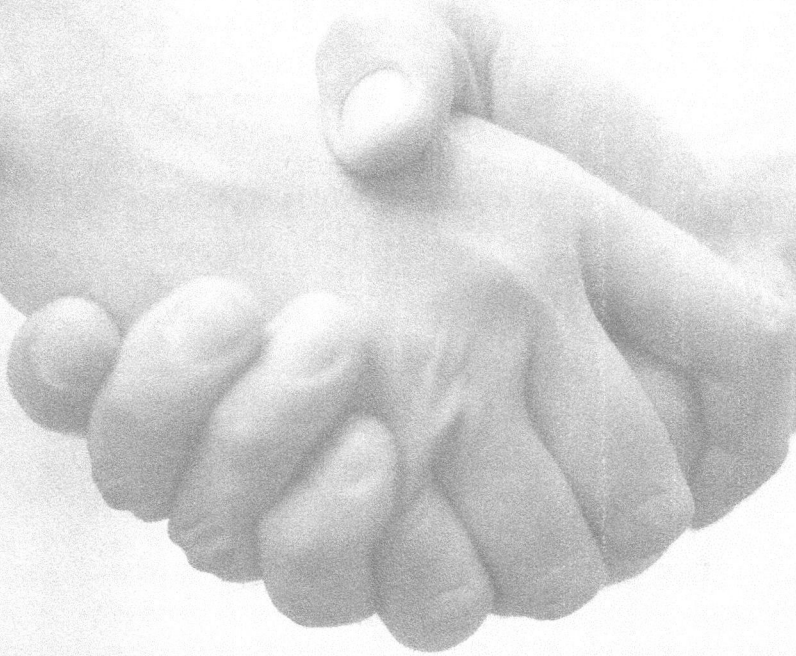

When you have a vision for your life or a dream that you are working towards, it gives you a greater sense of purpose and a natural energy that is unexplainable.

READING TIME

As you read
Chapter 9:
"The Choice
of Vision" in
HANDSHAKE,
reflect on the
questions and
scriptures.

REFLECT AND TAKE ACTION:

What stands out to you from Bill Gates's vision for Microsoft in this chapter?

_____

_____

_____

_____

_____

_____

_____

_____

_____

_____

_____

_____

What is your vision for your life? For your organization? For your family?

_____

_____

_____

_____

_____

_____

_____

_____

_____

_____

_____

What four things does vision do for you? List them and briefly describe each.

I. _____

_____

2. _____

_____

3. _____

_____

4. _____

_____

Have you ever worked for a leader with a big vision? How did this affect your work?

_____

_____

_____

_____

_____

_____

_____

_____

_____

What do you do to keep your vision at the forefront of your mind?

_____

_____

_____

_____

_____

_____

_____

_____

_____

What are some things that tend to distract you from your vision?

_____

_____

_____

_____

_____

_____

_____

_____

_____

What area of your life needs a vision? Take time to create a vision statement using the steps provided in this chapter.

_____

_____

_____

_____

_____

_____

_____

_____

_____

CHAPTER 10

THE CHOICE OF EXCELLENCE

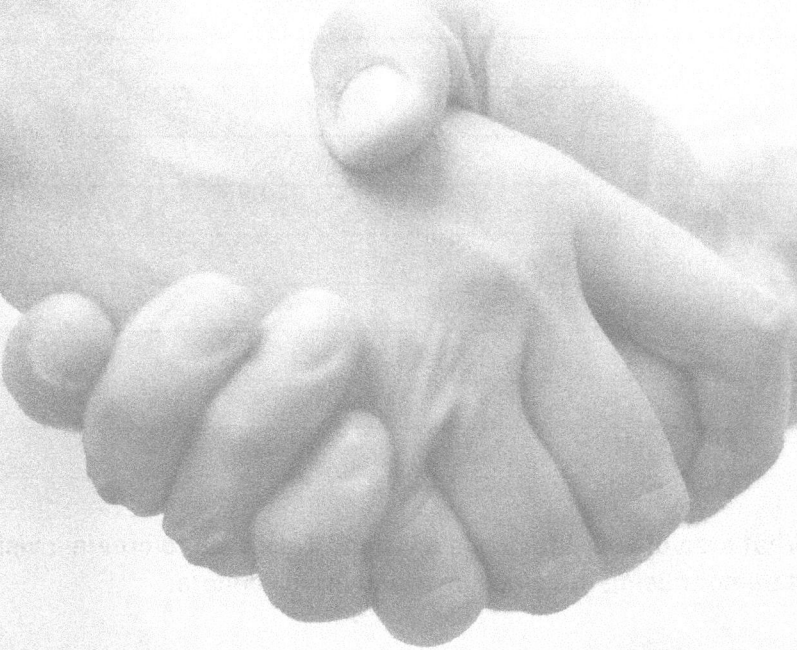

Regardless of how successful you
have been, excellence is the ingredient
that will take you even higher.

READING TIME

As you read Chapter 10: "The Choice of Excellence" in HANDSHAKE, reflect on the questions and scriptures.

REFLECT AND TAKE ACTION:

How do you define "excellence"? What would excellence look like in your current position?

_____

_____

_____

_____

_____

_____

_____

_____

_____

Have you ever fallen into one of the negative ways of thinking that inhibits excellence? Which? How did you combat this perspective?

_____

_____

_____

_____

_____

_____

_____

_____

_____

_____

How is excellence different from perfection? Should we pursue both? Why or why not?

_____

_____

_____

_____

_____

_____

_____

Have your emotions ever inhibited your ability to pursue excellence? How?

_____

_____

_____

_____

_____

_____

What areas of your life do you currently strive for excellence in? What areas do you need to try harder in?

_____

_____

_____

_____

_____

_____

_____

What are some things you can strategically place in your personal life or your organization that will help you achieve excellence?

_____

_____

_____

_____

_____

_____

_____

What small adjustments in your home, work, or life can you make today that will move you closer to excellence?

_____

_____

_____

_____

_____

_____

_____

What have you taken away from this study guide that you can implement immediately?

_____

_____

_____

_____

_____

_____

_____

www.ingramcontent.com/pod-product-compliance
Lightning Source LLC
Chambersburg PA
CBHW070051100426
42734CB00040B/2979